WORLD WAR II

BATTLES OF WORLD WAR II

Mike Taylor

Visit us at
www.abdopub.com

Published by Abdo Publishing Company, 4940 Viking Drive, Edina, MN 55435.
Copyright ©1998 by Abdo Consulting Group, Inc. International copyrights
reserved in all countries. No part of this book may be reproduced in any form
without written permission from the publisher.

Printed in the United States.

Graphic Design: John Hamilton
Contributing Editors: Alan Gergen; John Hamilton; Morgan Hughes
Cover photo: Digital Stock
Interior photos: Digital Stock

Sources: Churchill, Winston S. *The Second World War.* 6 vols., New York, 1948-
1953; Stokesbury, James L. *A Short History of World War II.* New York, William
Morrow and Company, 1980; Weinberg, Gerhard. *A World At Arms, a Global
History of World War II.* Cambridge University Press, 1994; Wright, Gordon. *The
Ordeal of Total War, 1939-1945.* New York: Harper & Row, 1968.

Library of Congress Cataloging–in–Publication Data

Taylor, Mike.
    Battles of World War II / Mike Taylor
        p. cm. — (World War II)
    Includes index.
    Summary: Describes the battles of World War II which show the early
successes of the Axis powers and then the gradual triumph of the Allies.
    ISBN 1-56239-804-0
    1. World War, 1939-1945—Juvenile literature. 2. Battles—History—20th
century—Juvenile literature. [1. World War, 1939-1945. 2. Battles.]
I. Title. II. Series: World War II (Edina, Minn.)
D743.7.T36   1998
940.53—dc21   98-4807
                                                        CIP
                                                        AC

CONTENTS

U.S. Marines at Cape Totkina on Bougainville, Solomon Islands.

THE BATTLE OF POLAND

World War II was fought between 1939 and 1945. Germany, Italy, and Japan began the war because they hoped to expand their empires. Together, Germany, Italy and Japan were called the Axis powers. Great Britain and the United States led a large group of countries to resist the Axis powers. These countries were called the Allies.

During the first half of the war, the Axis powers won their battles regularly. The German *Blitzkrieg* strategy worked perfectly. After 1941, when the United States entered the war against Japan and Germany, the Allies began to turn the tide. The battles described in this book show the early successes of the Axis powers, and then the gradual triumph of the Allies.

World War II began officially on September 1, 1939, when the German army, the *Wehrmacht*, invaded the neighboring country of Poland. Germany had claimed for many years that parts of northern Poland were rightfully German territory because many German-speaking people lived there alongside the Poles. The Polish government insisted that the territory belonged to Poland and vowed to defend it. When Germany finally launched its invasion, France and Great Britain promised to help Poland and immediately declared war on Germany.

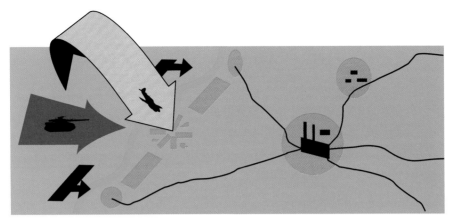

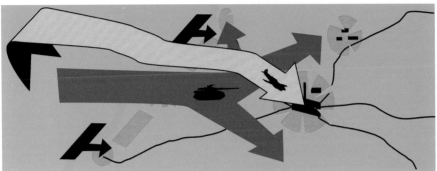

The Battle of Poland was very important because it gave the world its first glimpse of the powerful German *Blitzkrieg* strategy. The German word *Blitzkrieg* means "lightning warfare." *Blitzkrieg* strategy calls for very large and fast-moving attacks that overwhelm the enemy quickly and completely. German leaders hoped that *Blitzkrieg* would allow them to avoid the kind of long, drawn-out battles that led to Germany's defeat in World War I.

In a *Blitzkrieg* attack, the German army used its numerous tanks to break small holes through the enemy lines. Its fighter aircraft and Junkers 87 (also called Stukas) dive bombers would destroy railroads and highways so that the enemy troops could not move around easily to fill the holes. Finally, the infantry, or foot soldiers, would pour through the holes in large numbers to surround the enemy army from the rear.

In a *Blitzkrieg* attack, aircraft and armored units pierce the center as infantry units keep defenders busy along the length of the battle front (above). Once the center has been pierced (below), the armored spearhead fans out and cuts off the enemy's supply lines, also attacking from the rear.

Blitzkrieg strategy worked perfectly against Poland during the first two weeks of September 1939. Two German armies attacked Poland, first with tanks and aircraft to break through the Polish defense, then with infantry to surround the Polish army from the rear.

German fighter airplanes shot up Polish transport trains and airports while Stuka dive bombers terrorized Polish civilians in the cities and relied on their agility to perform precise bombing missions. Stukas were outfitted with special sirens to make them more frightening. Special German bombers flew over Poland to parachute thousands of dummies dressed in Polish uniforms. This was supposed to discourage the real Polish soldiers who would be tricked into believing that their comrades had joined the enemy.

A German Stuka dive bomber.

The Polish weapons were inferior in every way. The Poles had no tanks and were baffled by the new high-speed tanks in the German *Blitzkrieg*. Indeed, the strength of the Polish army was its horsed cavalry, rightly described by Polish generals as the best in the world. Sadly, Polish soldiers on horses, armed with swords, were no match for German tanks.

The *Blitzkrieg* in Poland lasted for two weeks before the Germans had surrounded the Polish army. The German treatment of the Polish people after 1939 was one of the most barbaric aspects of World War II. Polish civilians were enslaved or killed outright while the German army stole everything of value throughout the country. The world's first glimpse of the German *Blitzkrieg* was a grim one, indeed, and struck fear into people around the world.

THE BATTLE FOR FRANCE

Although France and Great Britain declared war on Germany during the Battle of Poland and vowed to help liberate Poland, they did not confront Germany immediately. Weak political leadership during recent years had left both countries unprepared for war. Thus, while Germany attacked Denmark and Norway, France and Great Britain spent the winter of 1939-1940 stockpiling weapons and training troops. Journalists in France and Great Britain called this winter the "Phony War," because there was very little fighting against Germany even though they had declared war.

France put the finishing touches on its great defensive system called the Maginot Line. The Maginot Line was a long line of fortresses along the border between France and Germany all the way from Switzerland in the south to the Ardennes Forest in the

A scout runs for cover on a battlefield in Belgium.

north. The line was armed with countless heavy cannons and rapid-fire machine guns. It was protected with barbed wire and mine fields.

The French had made one fatal miscalculation in the construction of the Maginot Line. The French stopped the line at the Ardennes Forest in the north. They believed that Germany could not drive tanks through the steep and narrow roads in the forest. However, when the Germans finally attacked France on May 10, 1940, German tanks simply drove around the Maginot Line, proving that they could pass through the Ardennes Forest easily and quickly. The Maginot Line proved to be one of the biggest military failures in history.

Meanwhile, the German *Blitzkrieg* strategy worked as well in France as it had in Poland. The French hoped the Germans would be stopped by the great fortress Eben Emael in Belgium. Eben Emael was a state-of-the-art fortress constructed from hardened concrete with steel reinforcement. But specially trained German commandos piloted glider aircraft onto Eben Emael's roof on May 14, 1940. Armed with dynamite and machine guns, the commandos exploded holes in the roof and overran the great fortress in one day.

A week later Germany's great tank commanders, Heinz Guderian and Erwin Rommel, surrounded the best part of the French and British armies in northern France. There were nearly a million British and French soldiers trapped in the port town of Dunkirk, certain of capture by the Germans. Declaring an emergency, the British navy called for every available vessel to help rescue the two armies. Hundreds of ships of every type, including fishing boats and sailboats, were used to save the men and transport them to safety in Great Britain, 30 miles across the English Channel. Journalists called this event the "Miracle at Dunkirk."

Despite the happy news, the world was horrified by the quick defeat of France. Newspapers published photographs of the *Blitzkrieg* in France. People saw French civilians fleeing before German tanks and Stuka dive bombers. It seemed to the whole world that Germany was about to win the war.

A Frenchman weeps as German soldiers march into Paris.

THE BATTLE OF BRITAIN

The first mass air raid on London, England.

The quick defeat in France had proven that both France and Great Britain were poorly prepared for the war. The lack of preparation was blamed on the political leaders in both countries, and the people chose new leaders immediately. In Great Britain, Winston Churchill was chosen to replace Neville Chamberlain as prime minister, the most powerful political leader in the country. Winston Churchill was already famous for his exciting speeches and his patriotism. It was hoped that Churchill could inspire the British people to stand up to the Germans alone.

Churchill correctly predicted that Germany would quickly turn against Great Britain after it had finished off France. The British installed brand new technology called radar along their southern coastline. Radar uses sound waves to determine the location of objects in the air. British scientists predicted it could be used to detect German bombers long before they crossed the English Channel into British territory.

The German bomber attack began in August 1940, when the Luftwaffe sent 485 bomber and 1,000 fighter plane missions across the English Channel. Churchill's careful management ensured that British factories could build planes faster than Germany was able to shoot them down. With radar, British pilots could attack German planes far out over the English Channel. With high-speed Spitfire fighter planes, British pilots destroyed German planes much faster than German factories could replace them.

A British RAF Spitfire fighter plane.

Even with the great tension during the Battle of Britain, Churchill worked to ensure the safety and survival of his pilots. For example, Churchill insisted that every pilot be given a new flying suit specially designed to keep the pilot dry and warm if his plane were shot down over the water. Most British pilots parachuted into the water and, with the new flying suits, stayed alive to be rescued by navy ships.

Churchill gave all credit to his beloved pilots. In one of his most famous speeches, Churchill praised Britain's pilots as heroes: "Never in the field of human conflict was so much owed by so many to so few."

Despite the success of radar and the efforts of the British pilots, many German bombers managed to reach their targets in London and other cities. German bombers worked especially hard to bomb British airports and aircraft factories in order to stop Britain from building any new planes to replace those that were shot down. Churchill's speeches inspired the

English people to continue their resistance to the Germans. Factory workers continued to work despite the severe danger and food shortages. In another famous speech Churchill praised the British people: "If the British empire and its commonwealth last for a thousand years, men still will say 'this was their finest hour.'"

By the end of September 1940, nearly two months after the Battle of Britain had begun, German leader Adolf Hitler called off the attack. Germany was losing too many planes and had no chance of winning. Churchill became a hero worldwide for his fierce leadership during the darkest days of the battle.

Despite hits from German bombs, London's St. Paul's Cathedral survived.

PEARL HARBOR

American President Franklin Roosevelt did not wish to involve the United States in the war. But Japanese hostility to its neighboring countries offended Roosevelt and the U.S. government. The United States imposed an oil embargo on Japan. This meant that Japan could buy no oil for its factories and navy. President Roosevelt and others hoped this would prevent further Japanese expansion.

Japan retaliated for the oil embargo with a surprise attack on Pearl Harbor, a U.S. naval base in Hawaii. On the morning of December 7, 1941, Japanese aircraft carriers moved within range of Pearl Harbor. The United States had radar and knew that the Japanese planes were coming. However, poor management led them to believe that these were American planes arriving from California.

The USS *Arizona* burns and sinks after the Japanese attack on Pearl Harbor.

Japanese airplanes and submarines wrecked 5 American battleships in the first 20 minutes. The battleship *Oklahoma* capsized immediately. The *West Virginia* managed to stay upright and settle in shallow water so that it could continue firing its guns. Tragically, the *Arizona* was hit by a torpedo so that its own ammunition exploded in a massive fireball. The burning wreck of the *Arizona* sank with more than 1,000 sailors trapped inside. A memorial has been built in Pearl Harbor to mark the spot where the *Arizona* sank and to honor the sailors who died.

President Roosevelt condemned the Japanese treachery and explained that the United States must now join the war against Japan and Germany. Despite the short-term success, the Japanese attack on Pearl Harbor proved to be a long-term error. The United States Navy recovered quickly. The United States immediately brought new weapons, new manpower, and new enthusiasm into the war against Japan and the other Axis powers.

An airfield at Pearl Harbor is attacked by Japanese dive bombers.

MIDWAY AND GUADALCANAL

The war between the United States and Japan in the Pacific Ocean was the first time in history that large numbers of aircraft carriers were used in battle. These were monster ships, some as long as a football field, with elevators to lift the planes up from below deck onto the runway. The range of their aircraft allowed them to do battle with other carriers at great distances, often not even within sight of each other.

Seven months after the disastrous attack on Pearl Harbor, the United States managed a tremendous victory over Japan in the Battle of Midway. On June 4, 1942, American pilots discovered a large fleet of Japanese ships heading toward the Midway Islands, a small group between Hawaii and Japan. As American planes attacked the Japanese fleet, Japanese planes attacked the American carriers, hoping to destroy them before the American planes returned.

A SB2C dive bomber gets set to land on the USS *Yorktown.*

The battle lasted for two days. By June 6 the American victory was sealed. In the end Japan lost four aircraft carriers and numerous other large warships. The United States lost only one aircraft carrier, the *Yorktown*, which had been damaged earlier in the Battle of the Coral Sea and was now sunk. As in the Battle of the Coral Sea, the opposing fleets, dominated by huge aircraft carriers, fought the entire battle without ever coming into sight of one another.

The victory turned the war in the Pacific to the favor of the United States. The Japanese continued to fight relentlessly, but the United States had stopped their advances to the south, toward Australia, and to the east, toward Hawaii. Having stopped the Japanese advance, the United States now prepared to push Japan backward out of the island strongholds it had captured during the first year of the war.

Many of the battles fought while pushing Japan back were small but harsh fights on the beaches and in the jungles of the South Pacific islands. U.S. Marines fought against diseases and desperate Japanese soldiers in sweltering heat and pouring rainstorms. Oftentimes the Japanese soldiers dug secure forts into the earth and waited for the Marines to attack. A few Japanese soldiers armed only with machine guns could stop hundreds of Marines under these circumstances.

The Battle of Guadalcanal was the first such battle. Guadalcanal is one of the Solomon Islands in the South Pacific. It was very important to the Japanese because it was large enough to build a substantial airfield. With an airfield, Guadalcanal could be used to defend all of the surrounding islands. If the U.S. Marines were to capture the island, Japanese leaders feared, they would be able to position American bombers dangerously close to Japan itself.

Jungle warfare in the South Pacific.

Indeed, the United States attacked Guadalcanal in August. U.S. Marines waded ashore onto the beaches despite machine gun fire from the Japanese. The battle raged for a month. The Marines captured an airfield and renamed it Henderson Field. The high ground around the field was nicknamed "Bloody Ridge." While the Japanese tried to occupy Bloody Ridge and recapture the airfield, the Marines held them off with mortars and large cannons called howitzers.

Gradually, during October and November 1942, the U.S. Navy managed to take control of the waters surrounding Guadalcanal. This prevented the Japanese from sending food and ammunition to their troops on the island, now cut off and surrounded. Finally, in February 1943, a small Japanese fleet sneaked past the U.S. Navy for a daring rescue of the Japanese survivors trapped on the island.

Although the Japanese fleet rescued 11,000 soldiers, the Battle of Guadalcanal was clearly a victory for the United States. With the planes of Henderson Field to protect them, U.S. warships dominated the entire area. Although the Battle of Guadalcanal had cost thousands of American lives, the Japanese Empire had been dealt a decisive defeat.

TIMELINE OF THE GREAT BATTLES

1939 *September*: Battle of Poland. German *Blitzkrieg* overwhelms Poland with high-speed tanks and aircraft. The Battle of Poland was the beginning of World War II.

November 1939—May 1940: The Phony War. Britain and France declare war on Germany, but the fight doesn't start until May 1940.

1940 *August—September:* Battle of Britain. Britain uses newly invented radar units and fighter airplanes to intercept German bombers. The Battle of Britain was the largest air battle in World War II.

1941 *December 7:* Surprise attack on Pearl Harbor. Japanese aircraft carriers stage successful surprise attack and destroy much of the American fleet at Pearl Harbor in Hawaii. Because the Japanese used strict radio silence, it was impossible for the Americans to intercept messages and predict the attack.

1942 *June:* Battle of Midway. One of the greatest battles among aircraft carriers. Japanese aircraft carriers attacked, but the Americans were prepared and won the battle decisively. The Americans sank four Japanese aircraft carriers. The Japanese sank one American carrier, the *Yorktown*.

1942 *August 7:* Battle of Guadalcanal. U.S. Marines use landing craft to invade and capture this important island from the Japanese.

1942-43 *Winter*: Battle of Stalingrad. Germans and Soviets engage in street-to-street and building-to-building battle for the Soviet city of Stalingrad. Small machine guns were very important to this style of fighting. In February 1943 the surviving Germans ran out of ammunition and supplies and were forced to surrender. German and Soviet losses totalled nearly half a million soldiers.

1944 *June 6:* D-Day. Allied forces use hundreds of small landing craft to attack the beaches of northern France. The Allies landed so many soldiers in this way that they eventually liberated Paris and pushed the Germans out of France.

1945 *May 8:* V-E Day. Victory in Europe! The Germans surrender to American General Dwight D. Eisenhower.

1945 *August 6:* Hiroshima. American bomber *Enola Gay* drops an atomic bomb on the Japanese city of Hiroshima. Around 130,000 Japanese civilians are killed or seriously injured. Three days later, on August 9, another atomic bomb is dropped on the city of Nagasaki.

1945 *August 14:* Japanese surrender. Japan surrenders to the Allies after witnessing the terrible destruction in the cities of Hiroshima and Nagasaki. The surrender documents are signed by Japanese representatives aboard the USS *Missouri*.

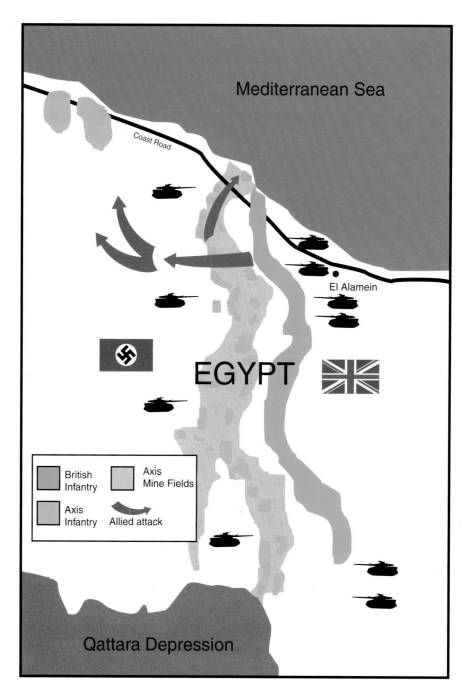

The Battle of El Alamein, Egypt, was fought on a narrow stretch of land bounded by the Mediterranean Sea and the Qattara Depression.

STALINGRAD AND EL ALAMEIN

Just as the United States had turned the war against Japan, so were the Allies turning the war against Germany. First, the British stopped the Germans at the Battle of El Alamein in August 1942. Then, the Soviet Union defeated a large German army at the Soviet city of Stalingrad in January 1943. These two battles together were the first major defeats suffered by Germany.

In 1941, German leader Adolf Hitler summoned his most respected tank commander, General Erwin Rommel, to command a new desert army in North Africa. Rommel quickly became notorious for his brilliant leadership in the desert war and earned the nickname the "Desert Fox."

Rommel's British enemies had their tricks as well. During the summer of 1942 the British retreated all the way to the town of El Alamein in Egypt. They surrendered much territory to Rommel's troops.

However, the British position at El Alamein was a good one. Just outside the town lie the great Qattara Depression. The Qattara Depression was a huge, impassable rock canyon. It was impossible to drive or march through it. Rommel would have to attack through the very narrow lane of safe ground between the Qattara Depression and the Mediterranean Sea. This would make defense much simpler for the British forces.

The British commander in El Alamein, General Bernard Montgomery, played his cards perfectly. British spies had broken the German code. They informed Montgomery of Rommel's moves in advance. Indeed, to the amazement of his troops, Montgomery picked the exact time and place of Rommel's attack on El Alamein. British tanks and aircraft were lying in wait when Rommel attacked on August 30, 1942, nearly two months after he first launched attacks on British positions in hopes of capturing Cairo and the Suez Canal.

Rommel's attack failed miserably, and while he retreated to reorganize, Montgomery prepared for a large counter-attack. The counter-attack began on October 24. Nine hundred British cannons bombarded Rommel's men for two days. Still Rommel's forces did not retreat. Finally, on November 5, 1942, after several unsuccessful counter-attacks, the "Desert Fox" admitted defeat and began to flee westward. His army was exhausted and short of ammunition. They had to abandon trucks and even tanks as they fled because they had no more fuel. By January 1943, the British had been joined by the U.S. Army in North Africa. The combined armies, with new weapons and fresh soldiers, cooperated to force Germany out of North Africa altogether.

Meanwhile, the Soviet Union was successfully turning the war against Germany in Europe. Germany had invaded the Soviet Union in June 1941 with the hope of a quick *Blitzkrieg* battle that would force the Soviets to surrender before winter.

However, the *Blitzkrieg* did not work in the Soviet Union. The winter came early, paralyzing the German army in the snow and cold. Planning for a *Blitzkrieg,* the confident German soldiers did not even bother to carry winter clothes or boots with them. They expected to win the battle quickly during the summer.

German infantry fighting in Russia.

After surviving the first winter, the Germans were ready to move again by June. Hitler's goal was to capture the city of Stalingrad, named after Soviet leader Josef Stalin. Hitler believed that capturing the city named after Stalin would demoralize Soviet people and bring them to surrender. Instead, the Soviet army defended Stalingrad stubbornly.

In November 1942, German General Friedrich von Paulus found his army surrounded in Stalingrad with the Soviet army moving closer every day.

For weeks, the German air force was able to parachute food and ammunition in to Paulus and his army. However, as the winter set in, the flights became impossible, and Paulus ran short of supplies.

In December the Soviet army moved in on the Germans. The Germans were hungry and cold, but fought desperately in Stalingrad. Much of the city was destroyed in the street-to-street combat. Many German troops starved and froze to death. Finally, in January 1943, just as Rommel was being defeated in North Africa, General Paulus surrendered to the Soviet army.

The Battle of Stalingrad was an important victory for the Soviets. Over 200,000 Germans were killed, either by the fighting or by hunger or cold. Another 91,000 were captured and sent to prison in the Soviet Union. (Less than 5,000 returned home alive after the war.) After the victory at Stalingrad, the Soviet army pushed the Germans slowly back to the west.

A German trooper's face shows the misery of winter fighting in the Soviet Union.

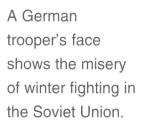

THE D-DAY INVASION

After the great Allied victories of 1942 and 1943, President Roosevelt and Prime Minister Winston Churchill planned to liberate France from German domination in 1944. The Allies would attack on the beaches of Normandy in northern France.

General Dwight Eisenhower confers with his troops before the D-Day invasion.

The great Allied attack began on June 6, 1944. The day was named "D-Day" by military planners, and the invasion was code-named "Operation Overlord." Operation Overlord was the largest invasion of its kind in history. Nearly three million men, with thousands of ships and airplanes, took part. American General Dwight Eisenhower was named as the supreme commander of the huge force.

Large ships transported the troops across the stormy English Channel. Then the men were loaded into much smaller boats called landing craft. The landing craft moved the men into shallow water, where they waded ashore. Many men became seasick as the waves tossed the tiny landing craft about.

There were no docks present where the transport ships could unload the tons of necessary supplies. Many of the ships brought their own docks with them! They towed huge barges behind them and sank them near the beaches. The sunken barges were code-named "Mulberries" and they worked very well as docks.

The Germans defending the beaches of Normandy were commanded by General Erwin Rommel, who had been relocated after his defeat in North Africa. For a while, the Germans were able to hold off the British and American attackers. Gradually, however, Allied bombers forced the Germans to pull back and make way for the thousands of Allied troops wading ashore.

The beaches were very dangerous and thousands of young men were killed on the first day. But after three weeks Eisenhower had assembled almost one million soldiers on the French shore, mostly French, Canadian,

Under heavy fire, American troops wade ashore during the D-Day invasion.

American and British. They prepared quickly to attack inland.

At the end of July the attackers began to move inland, pushing the Germans in front of them. The American Third Army, under the command of General George Patton, dashed forward using its tanks brilliantly. In August the Allies liberated Paris, the capital city of France. By winter the Americans had pushed almost all the way to the German border.

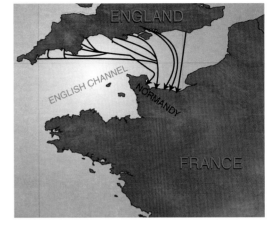

The Allied D-Day invasion of Normandy, France.

The D-Day invasion was a tremendous success. The Germans attacked once more in December in the Ardennes Forest. This brief but brutal battle lasted from December 16 until December 23, and is known as the Battle of the Bulge. After defeating the Germans at the Battle of the Bulge, American forces crossed the Rhine River into Germany, certain of victory. Meanwhile the Soviet army had liberated Poland and was closing in on Berlin, the capital city of Germany.

With his army crumbling around him, German leader Adolf Hitler committed suicide on April 30, 1945. The German army surrendered a week later and the Allies declared May 8, 1945, to be V-E Day, for Victory in Europe.

On August 6, the United States dropped an atomic bomb on the Japanese city of Hiroshima. On August 9, another atomic bomb was dropped on Nagasaki. The destruction was devastating. Facing certain defeat, the Japanese government surrendered on August 14, 1945.

CONCLUSION

Wars bring out the worst and the best in people. Great crimes were committed against helpless victims like the Jews of Eastern Europe and the sailors of the battleship *Arizona*. However, there were many heroes as well. It is important to remember the brave U.S. Marines who fought the difficult island battles in the South Pacific, the Soviet troops who defended Stalingrad despite hunger and bitter cold, and the great Allied forces that waded ashore on D-Day at Normandy. All contributed to the Allied victory over the Axis powers.

A French tribute to a fallen American soldier.

INTERNET SITES

A-Bomb WWW Museum
http://www.csi.ad.jp/ABOMB/index.html
    This site provides readers with accurate information concerning the impact of the first atomic bomb on Hiroshima, Japan.

Black Pilots Shatter Myths
http://www.af.mil/news/features/features95/f_950216-112_95feb16.html
    This site tells of the exploits of the 332nd Fighter Group, the first all-black flying unit known as the Tuskegee Airmen.

United States Holocaust Museum
http://www.ushmm.org/
    The official Web site of the U.S. Holocaust Memorial Museum in Washington, D.C.

What Did You Do In The War, Grandma?
http://www.stg.brown.edu/projects/WWII_Women/tocCS.html
    An oral history of Rhode Island women during World War II. In this project, 17 students interviewed 36 Rhode Island women who recalled their lives in the years before, during, and after the Second World War.

World War II Commemoration
http://www.grolier.com/wwii/wwii_mainpage.html
    To commemorate the 50th anniversary of the end of the war, Grolier Online assembled a terrific collection of World War II historical materials on the Web. Articles taken from *Encyclopedia Americana* tell the story of World War II, including biographies. Also included are combat films, photographs, a World War II history test, and links to many other sites.

These sites are subject to change. Go to your favorite search engine and type in "World War II" for more sites.

Pass It On
    World War II buffs: educate readers around the country by passing on information you've learned about World War II. Share your little-known facts and interesting stories. We want to hear from you! To get posted on the ABDO & Daughters website, E-mail us at "History@abdopub.com"

Visit the ABDO & Daughters website at www.abdopub.com

 29

GLOSSARY

Blitzkrieg: German word meaning "lightning warfare." Describes a new German military strategy in World War II. *Blitzkrieg* called for very large invasions to overwhelm the enemy quickly and avoid long, drawn out battles.

Stuka: A type of German dive bomber. Stukas could carry as much as 1,000 pounds of bombs. They were very frightening to people because they were so loud and because the Germans had so many of them. They worked to frighten people into submission.

Maginot Line: Named after the French general who invented the idea, the Maginot Line was a long line of fortresses along the border between France and Germany. The Maginot Line was considered to be absolutely safe and secure. In May 1940 German tanks simply went around the line, through the Ardennes Forest to the north. The Maginot Line proved to be one of the largest military failures in history.

Miracle of Dunkirk: The British navy rescued nearly one million trapped soldiers from certain capture in northern France during May 1940.

Winston Churchill: Prime minister of Great Britain during World War II. He was very famous for his patriotic speeches and fierce resistance to the Germans.

Franklin Roosevelt: President of the U.S. during World War II.

D-Day, June 6, 1944: Code name for the beginning of the great Allied attack on German forces in France.

V-E Day, May 8, 1945: After German leader Adolf Hitler committed suicide, the German generals surrendered on May 7. The United States proclaimed May 8 to be "V-E Day," which stood for "Victory in Europe."

Hiroshima: Name of the Japanese city where the United States dropped the first atomic bomb, on August 6, 1945. The city was destroyed.

Pilots on an F6F Hellcat on board the USS *Lexington*.

INDEX